Parents~Passing
the Torch
of Faith

Other Books by the Author

Bringing Your Family Together in Prayer
Abbey Press, 1993

Doing What Comes Spiritually
Herald Press, 1993

For the Love of Marriage
Good Books, 1996

If I Were Starting My Family Again
Good Books, 1994

If I Were Starting My Ministry Again
Abingdon Press, 1995

Meditations for the Newly Married
Herald Press, 1995

Now Is the Time to Love
Herald Press, 1970

Seven Things Children Need
Herald Press, 1988

When Your Child Is 6 to 12
Good Books, 1994

Parents~Passing the Torch of Faith

John M. Drescher

Herald
Press

Scottdale, Pennsylvania
Waterloo, Ontario

Library of Congress Cataloging-in-Publication Data
Drescher, John M.
    Parents—passing the torch of faith / John M. Drescher.
      p. cm.
    "Parts of chapters 1-3 first appeared in Christian living,
autumn 1996, pp. 33-35."—T.p. verso.
    Includes bibliographical references (p.).
    ISBN 0-8361-9076-9 (alk. paper)
    1. Family—Religious life. 2. Christian education—Home
training. 3. Parenting—Religious aspects—Christianity.
I. Title.
BV4526.2.D734 1997
248.8'45—dc21
                                       97-13311

Bible texts are used by permission, all rights reserved, and unless otherwise noted are from the *New Revised Standard Version Bible,* copyright 1989, by the Division of Christian Education of the National Council of the Churches of Christ in the USA; JB, from *The Jerusalem Bible*, copyright © 1966 by Darton, Longman & Todd, Ltd. and Doubleday, a division of Bantam, Doubleday, Dell Publishing Group, Inc. KJV, from the King James Version.

Parts of chapters 1-3 first appeared in *Christian Living*, autumn 1996, pp. 33-35.

PARENTS—PASSING THE TORCH OF FAITH
Copyright © 1997 by Herald Press, Scottdale, Pa. 15683
    Published simultaneously in Canada by Herald Press,
    Waterloo, Ont. N2L 6H7. All rights reserved
Library of Congress Catalog Number: 97-13311
International Standard Book Number: 0-8361-9076-9
Printed in the United States of America
Book and cover design by Merrill R. Miller

06 05 04 03 02 01 00 99 98 97 10 9 8 7 6 5 4 3 2 1

*To all families
who seek to pass on
the torch of faith*

Contents

Preface

"We always are only one generation from heathen-dom." If one generation fails to pass on the torch of faith, the next generation will not recognize God and will live in ignorance of his will. It's as simple as that.

The proof is all around us. We don't want the sad story of Judges 2:10 to happen on our watch: "Another generation grew up after them, who did not know the Lord or the work that he had done for Israel."

Many Christian parents want help, not only in the educational, emotional, and physical care of children, but also for guidance in giving spiritual direction. Much of the momentum for home schooling comes from concern for the spiritual dimension, so often missing in society, schools, and even church life.

These are testing times. Many parents and youth are getting their morals and models more from TV, movies, sports heroes, and secular society than from home, church, and spiritual leaders.

As Christian parents, we have a primary *concern*. We want the faith we have accepted to be transmitted, passed on to our children and future generations. There is no greater desire we have for our children.

In his fine book *How to Really Love Your Child*, Ross Campbell writes, "It is amazing to me how some parents spend thousands of dollars and go to any length of political manipulation to make sure their child is well prepared educationally. And yet, for the most important preparation of all, for life's spiritual battles and finding meaning in life, a child is left to fend for himself and made easy prey to cultists." [1]

We Christian parents have a primary *charge*. God says, "Take this child, and bring this child up for me." We know that the test of example: "These words shall be in your heart." We remember the task of teaching: "You shall teach them diligently to your children." These are charges for which we will be held accountable. No one else can assume this responsibility. God himself places it in our hands as parents.

Christian parents need a primary *commitment*. We dare not pass on the torch of faith haphazardly. There must be a commitment which sets priorities in time, effort, and energy. This will mean placing the spiritual ahead of the material. It can be one of the most exciting and satisfying things we will ever do.

All this may overwhelm us. But God has promised to be with us. We can move forward with courage because God will guide us through our concern, charge, and commitment. These short chapters are written to encourage parents to pass on the torch of faith.

Build
Build, but not for today alone.
Build with such solid stone,
And enduring inner structure,
That in the years to come
Your children's children
Will see and touch
And say with honor and with love,
"These are the stones
Our parents laid.
This is the building
Our parents built."

—John M. Drescher

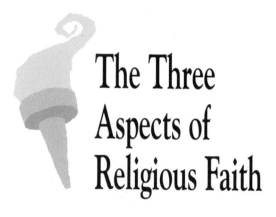

The Three Aspects of Religious Faith

Religious words have value to the child only as the child's experience in the home gives them meaning.
—Canon Lumb

*Little faces looking up
Holding wonder in a cup.*
—Sara Teasdale

Children do what adults do. . . . Life imitates life. Our children look to us for any limits of themselves.
—Christopher D. Vinck

The strongest incentives in the development of the character of children often come, not from direct and specific instruction, but from example and unargued assumptions.
—Elton Trueblood

1

Sensing Emotions and Attitudes

You shall love the Lord your God with all your heart, and with all your soul, and with all your might. Keep these words that I am commanding you today in your heart.
—Deuteronomy 6:5-6

Because it was raining outside, the children were playing in the living room while their mother was working in the kitchen. She heard the children's voices rising louder and louder. Finally she went to the living room door and scolded them for arguing.

She said, "That's not the way to act. Nobody is happy and helpful when you argue like that."

One of the little ones responded, "But, Mom, we aren't arguing. We're just playing Mom and Dad."

Emotional reactions attract children quickly. F. H. Richardson writes, "We know that [the child] . . . can and does unconsciously register parental tricks and habits and mannerisms at an age which seems impossible that he should be taking conscious note of his surroundings."[2]

Children learn about God through the parents' interpretation of life, as this relates to basic emotions and attitudes. Here is the first aspect of religious faith. The family's highest joys and deepest sorrows are expressed and experienced in the realities and responses of adults. The earliest feelings about God are formed in the family.

In the home we practice Christian faith in the most intimate way. The home is the basis of Christian nurture and the laboratory of daily life. Life is interpreted by the emotions and attitudes of father and mother toward each other and then toward others. In the family the child first feels and senses what is important. Here is the child's first view of life and its meaning.

The child begins to pick up our emotions and attitudes from birth, before the child can understand words. More students of human nature are saying that even prior to birth, the child is responding to parents' feelings and responses. From conception itself, the child absorbs feelings about life, spiritual things, and the sacred, as well as reverence for life, God, Scripture, other persons, and material things. Feelings play a crucial role in shaping a child.

Suppose a father is free to speak of sports, gets excited about sports, and attends sport activities. But if he shows little excitement about spiritual things and seldom speaks of them or sacrifices for them, the child senses his priorities.

If a mother gets enthused about her shopping spree but does not show equal enthusiasm for spiritual life, the child senses what is significant. Those attitudes and emotions deeply influence the child. We may later wonder why a child has little interest in spiritual things. We forget that the basic aspect of religious faith comes through constantly in our emotions and attitudes. The child is always filing them away for future reference.

Psychologists tell us that emotional attachment even more than instruction determines a weak or strong conscience. If emotional attachment is warm, loving, and caring, the child will develop a strong conscience. But if it is cold and distant, the child, no matter how much instruction is given, may develop a weak conscience and yield quickly to peer pressure.

Children are learners. They learn everywhere and at all times. They learn sitting down, walking, running, standing, even half-asleep. They are absorbing surfaces, taking in the impressions and expressions around them through their eyes, ears, fingers, feet, skin, imaginations, and feelings. They are learning when we wish them to—and when we wish they would not.

As Ralph Heynen says, "There is no place in life where the personal influence is stronger than in the family life. Parents will influence their children, whether they want to or not. It is only a question of what kind of heritage they will leave with them.

"It is not only a question of good and evil. Parents influence their children also through the emotional tone created in the home. When there are many tensions between the parents, or transferred from parents to children, these will also cast a shadow in which the children will walk, possibly all their days.

"I sometimes get the impression from people that they feel that the spiritual blessings are transferred in some mysterious way from parents to children. This is not so. Each parent stands as a link in that chain, and it depends upon the influence, the sense of values, the spiritual tone that is passed on from one generation to the next." [3]

Hence, parents need to cultivate their relationship with God and live in the joy of the Lord. If they give attention to keeping up their own spiritual and emotional health, they *will* influence their children for good.

Children will pick up and echo the parents' outlook on life, their emotional tone, and their spiritual sensibility. Thus children can grow into their parents' wholehearted love of God.

2

Modeling Appropriate Habits and Behavior

Set the believers an example in speech and conduct, in love, in faith, in purity. . . . Put these things into practice, devote yourself to them, so that all may see your progress. Pay close attention to yourself and to your teaching; continue in these things, for in doing this you will save both yourself and your hearers." —1 Timothy 4:12, 15-17

Here is the second aspect of religious faith. Parents always provide the primary models in their teaching of habits, behavior, and outlook on life.

A Congolese pastor told this story: All the fish in a nearby lake had a *nteke* or gathering. The elders had the children of all the fish swim past a reviewing stand. All of the fish children were applauded except those called *lokombe*, who swam on a slant. Their parents were mortified because their children had not done well.

When the *lokombe* children got home, they were scolded severely. They were too polite to explain the situation directly to their parents. They did, however, speak to some of the elders. These elders asked the children and their parents to swim by them. Of course, the parents also swam on a slant. The elders reproached the parents: "You can't expect your children to swim different from the way they see their parents swim."

Our children reflect a great deal about our Christian experience as parents. Few things impress children as much as the regard, excitement, and enjoyment parents and teachers have for everything which concerns God. Usually the child will develop real joy through imitating parents in this.

Moral values and respect for others, marriage, sanctity of sex, and all appropriate habits of behavior are caught even more than taught. We pass on our values of integrity, faithfulness, love, and honesty by demonstrating them in our lives as parents, spiritual leaders, and educators. We dare not be or do that which we do not want the child to be or do.

According to John Balguy, any parent who gives children good instructions and at the same time sets them a bad example is really "bringing them food in one hand and poison in the other."

A young man shared, "One of the earliest things I remember is making a Saturday night trip across town with Dad to return some money to a hardware dealer who had given him too much change. I'll never forget it."

It is no accident that Moses first commands parents

themselves to observe the Lord's commandments *diligently*. With such obedience showing every day, parents are in a position to teach their children with integrity (Deut. 6:3, 7).

A boy became treasurer of the Cub Scouts. After some time it was discovered he was pilfering money from the bag. When his dad found out, he gave his boy a severe scolding. The small boy defended himself: "But, Dad, that was only five dollars. I heard you say you beat the government out of $500 in income tax."

A recent study says 50 percent of college kids lie to parents. For example, they tell their parents books cost twice as much, so they have extra money. They report they were studying for a test when they were out partying. Seventy-seven percent of college students said they would lie to strangers.

I was in a Sunday school class of grandparents. No one challenged the statement that it is okay to lie under certain circumstances. We used to say "Let your 'Yes' be yes and your 'No' be no" (James 5:12; Matt. 5:37).

The parents' example is also the way the child learns stewardship of material things. Parents provide an example in giving, purchases made, and lifestyle. This sets the pattern for life.

As parents, we ought to read again and again for ourselves and for our children the book of Ecclesiastes. The Teacher pictures many paths people have taken down through the centuries to find meaning in life—possessions, pleasure, position, popularity. All end in vanity and vexation of spirit. The last two chapters end with the teaching that to save life, we give it away. We live not to get but to give, not to rule but to serve, not to keep but to sow bountifully. Happiness flows out of a pure and godly life.

Isn't it proved again and again? Why is suicide high among millionaires? In Sweden the people are provided physical and material comfort; so why is suicide a thousand times higher there than in Haiti? This is not to praise poverty but to warn that material things never satisfy.

Practices in the home also form habits of behavior. Currently there is little family prayer and Bible reading in homes, particularly among baby boomers, whose children are now in high school and college. Such lack may be a reaction against rigid forms of the past or simply a loss of any practice of prayer or reading of Scripture in the home or in personal life. Yet every spiritual awakening brings with it a renewal of family life and a return to family worship, study of Scripture, and prayer.

Many even neglect attending church and thus encouraging each other in the Christian faith (Heb. 10:25). Yet if our children think of worship only on Sunday, we are doomed. Life becomes divided into the secular and the sacred. George Buttrick wrote, "Just as six days of work each week in a false climate will ultimately destroy one hour of worship, however kindling, so forty hours of an indifferent home will quench the meaning of one hour in church."

A famous artist was particularly praised for his shades of blue. He never revealed his way of attaining that beautiful blue. The secret died with him and now can never be duplicated.

Likewise, the Christian faith is always one generation from extinction. The message is not lodged so much in books and documents as in human beings, particularly parents. Each generation must pass it on to the next generation or it is lost.

Surprisingly little space is given in Scripture to the subject of children. Since today we can read so many other books and articles on parent-child relationships, we are disappointed not to find more on this subject in the Bible. The Scriptures do urge parents to be the right kind of persons. The writers assume that, if this is true, children will grow up to love God and serve him.[4]

We are traveling home to God in the paths our parents trod. Many years ago Joshua made a declaration: "As for me and my household, we will serve the Lord" (Josh. 24:15). A home built on such a foundation may be shaken by storm, sickness, suffering, unemployment, and death. But it will not fail. It will pass on the torch of faith.

3

Teaching Our Beliefs

*But take care and watch yourself closely, so as neither to
forget the things that your eyes have seen nor to let them
slip from your mind all the days of your life; make them
known to your children and your children's children.*
—Deuteronomy 4:9

*You shall love the Lord your God with all your heart,
with all your soul, and with all your might. Keep these words
that I am commanding you today in your heart. Recite them
to your children.* —Deuteronomy 6:5-9

*And fathers, do not provoke your children to anger, but bring
them up in the discipline and instruction
of the Lord.* —Ephesians 6:4

According to Thomas Carlyle, the best thing that
ever happened to him was that he was obliged to learn

the Westminster Shorter Catechism. He had to master it thoroughly as a small child, though much of it he did not then understand. When he grew up, it kept erupting from him like a seasonal spring of water. When he came face to face with situations that tried his soul, those wonderful definitions of the catechism stared him in the face. He knew where he was.

The Holy Spirit uses the Scripture to bring conviction, cleansing, and guidance into our lives. The child who does not know Scripture is helpless, lacking guidance. The child who has the Scripture hidden in the heart as a treasure will be guided by the Holy Spirit (Ps. 119:11).

Here is the third and essential aspect of religious faith. It encompasses basic understandings of God, the universe, and life.

Our informal teaching

Our teaching is to be day by day and moment by moment. The Scripture has always pointed out that the teaching must be systematic, not hit-or-miss. Teaching is continuous when all of life is related to God's will—when we rise up, when we sit down, when we walk by the way, and when we go to bed at night (Deut. 6:7). God intends the warm circle of the family to be the habitat for nurture and protection of the child.

The child's faith should spring spontaneously from everyday life, joys, delights, and discoveries. Faith rises from the child's questions and secret desires, from the events of family and school life. Religious life must be alive and full of intent.

Religious stories can contribute much to a child's wonder of God, and so can short, vivid conversations on spiritual things. These should convey to the child the wealth of God's workings, with inexhaustible joys and unfailing attractions, and the Lord's call for loving response.

A salesperson in the picture department of a large store said, "Pictures are really holes in the wall of your home through which you can look out and see beauty."

G. Campbell Morgan, a great preacher in England, tells how early in marriage he and his wife invited his parents for a meal. As his parents were leaving, his father said, "Campbell, I don't see anything in your home which tells me you are a Christian."

Campbell admitted, "That's true."

His wife and he determined then and there that when a person entered their home, there would be something saying, "We are Christians."

One of the most natural ways to demonstrate our beliefs is through pictures we hang on the walls. Such visual delights should form part of the child's familiar world. Pictures can have a powerful impact in our teaching. They reveal the character of the people who live in the home, and shape the thoughts and imagination of those who dwell there or come for a visit.

I remember the story of the young man who was determined to go to sea. His parents wondered why he was so attracted to life on the sea.

One day, after the son had secured a position on a ship and left home, the mother sat in his room, thinking. Lifting her eyes, she saw a picture which had hung in her son's room since he was a small child. It showed a pilot, standing at the steering wheel of a ship during a severe storm. His face displayed courage and calm in the midst of the storm. Suddenly the mother realized the power that picture must have had on her son all his growing years.

So in a thousand ways, we can use the creation, as our Lord did, to call attention to God's infinite care, love, and provision. A true understanding of creation when the children are small can help in their understanding of life later on.

We need to read the Scriptures to our children. In our conversation, we can relate them to our children's lives. Other books on God's care and compassion can likewise be useful. We parents can help our children by pointing out how God is working in the lives of others. We can talk with God as a friend and relax in God's goodness.

Each day we can set a goal of reciting a little history of God's leading in life, telling how God delivers us physically and spiritually again and again. We don't need to answer a child's every question about the greatness and eternal nature of God. Instead, we can let our children live in the wonder that there are some things so great about God that even the wisest persons have never learned them.[5]

By age fifteen the average child has asked half a million questions. All these *what, why,* and *how* questions take us to the feet of God and are stirred by God to give parents opportunities to relate all life to him and his will. The child comes to believe what is talked about in the home.

This does not mean there should be constant chattering about religion. It means that teaching is to be constant, consistent, and concerned about the totality of life in relation to God and spiritual values.

By adolescence the child knows what parents believe and how they will respond in most situations. The child has felt and seen and heard it for twelve years. In their teen years, children ask themselves, "Will I adopt for myself what I have felt and seen and heard?"

Whether teenagers make an explicit response or not, they are more interested in what their parents think about questions of life than about what anyone else thinks.

Our formal teaching

Teaching is also to be formal, raising children in "the nurture and admonition of the Lord" (Eph. 6:4, KJV). That means giving instruction, correction, and guidance according to the child's needs. As the earliest scriptural instruction on child rearing says, the words which God commands shall be in the parents' heart, and they shall teach them *diligently* unto their children (Deut. 6:7, KJV).

A good surgeon uses a scalpel diligently. Parents must teach and guide to meet the needs of the child. Each child is different in need and response.

How do we do it? Let us go again to the Scripture. The Bible does not say, "When your children shall ask you, 'What do these ordinances and observations mean?' you shall say, 'Ask the preacher; he should have told you,' or 'Ask your Sunday school teacher or your teacher at your Christian school; they should know.' " That is what I call the *Reversed* Standard Version.

Instead, the Scripture tells parents to share the redemption story and its meaning in their lives. Here is the primary way of teaching and the charge God gives each parent, to pass on the torch of faith.

The early years of childhood provide opportunities to build a moral structure based on the principles which guide all life choices for the days and years ahead.

School and church, as important as they are, can never replace the power of example and instruction at home. Mother and father will always be the primary instructors of the child in morality and values. Those who fail to teach by example and word in the home cannot excuse themselves by blaming church, school, or community.

During the late nineteenth and early twentieth centuries, Scotland produced many great Christian preachers and teachers. The moral tone of the entire nation was lifted. The people were poor, but parents raised their children "on Proverbs and porridge," as some said.

In Proverbs we have the many contrasts of the way of the righteous and the way of the wicked. Proverbs bases wisdom solidly on the reverence of the Lord. When the reverence or fear of God is missing, wickedness will prevail.

What kind of harvest can we expect if children are raised on TV with its violence, moral perversions, and pernicious propaganda of false values? We must realize that what our children see and hear in the media is prepared by the most expert communicators of our day. They convey behavior, lifestyles, and morals which we Christian parents do not wish our children to adopt.

Today our children need our teaching. They need it beginning in the family, where God intends the great truths to be taught and to be illustrated. Scripture says that we need to talk and live our values when we get up in the morning, when we walk by the way, when we sit down, and when we go to bed (Deut. 6:7). In other words, teaching is a constant responsibility which we cannot expect anyone else to fulfill.

Psalm 78 gives important teaching about how we are to pass on the faith. Four generations are twice mentioned. Four overall truths are to be taught. There are seven results of such teaching.

Listen to this Law, my people,
pay attention to what I say;
I am going to speak to you in a parable
and expound the mysteries of our past.
Four Generations
What we have heard and known for ourselves,
and what our ancestors have told us,
must not be withheld from their descendants,
but be handed on by us to the next generation;
Four Things to Teach
that is; the titles of Yahweh, his power
and the miracles he has done.
When he issued the decrees for Jacob
and instituted a Law in Israel,

Four Generations

    He gave our ancestors strict orders
    to teach it to their children;
    the next generation was to learn it,
    the children still to be born,
    and these in turn were to tell their own children

Seven Results

    so that they too would put their confidence in God,
    never forgetting God's achievements,
    and always keeping his commandments,
    and not becoming like their ancestors,
    a stubborn and unruly generation,
    a generation with no sincerity of heart,
    in spirit unfaithful to God.

(Ps. 78:1-8, JB)

Parents are teachers without a holiday. The actions of our children which disturb us most are usually reflections of our own performance. Therefore, we should look honestly at ourselves. We must try to be real persons. We must avoid hypocrisy and put more emphasis on being the right examples.

We need to be alert to opportunities for direct teaching. But more, since most of our teaching is indirect and by example, and since we really are teaching all the time whether we want to or not, we must be on guard. Let us exercise self-control and be constantly dependent on divine help.

Years ago a mother wrote, "Do you ask what will educate your son? Your example will educate him; your conversation with your friends; the business he sees you transact; the likings and dislikings he sees you express—these will educate him. . . . Your . . . sta-

tion in life, your home, your table will educate him. . . .
Education goes on every instant of time; you neither
stop it nor turn its course. What these have a tendency
to make your child, that he will be all of his life."

These are the roles and functions assumed by families that no other institution can undertake. These are
the major roles and functions in passing on the faith.

"Whom will he teach knowledge, and to whom
will he explain the message? Those who are weaned
from milk, those taken from the breast? For it is precept upon precept, precept upon precept, line upon
line, line upon line, here a little, there a little" (Isa.
28:9-10).

As Evelyn Duvall says,

> Children learn to live, literally, in their families. It is here
> that the earliest relationships are established. It is in the
> family that emotional ties are forged and feelings are either expressed or repressed. It is in the family that children acquire an understanding of themselves, of others,
> and of life that serves them well or poorly. No other institution has ever been found in any time or clime that
> can approach the powerful influence of the family. [6]

Let us therefore regard our families as the greatest
schools on earth. We pass on the torch of faith as we
diligently observe the Lord's commandments and diligently teach our children, by precept and example.

4

Three Parables

I took a little child's hand in mine. He and I were to walk together for a while. I was to lead him to the Father. It was a task that overcame me, so awesome was the responsibility. I talked to the little child only of the Father. I painted the sternness of the Father's face, if the child were to displease him. We walked under tall trees. I said the Father had power to send them crashing down, struck by his thunderbolt. We walked in the sunshine. I told him of the greatness of the Father, who made the burning, blazing sun.

One twilight we met the Father. The child hid behind me; he was afraid; he would not look up at the loving face. He remembered my picture; he would not put his hand in the Father's hand. I was between the child and the Father. I wondered. I had been so conscientious, so serious.

*   *   *   *

I took a little child's hand in mine. I was to lead him to the Father. I felt burdened by the multitude of things I was to teach him. We did not ramble. We hastened on from spot to spot. At one moment we compared the leaves of the trees; in the next we were examining a bird's nest. While the child was questioning me about it, I hurried him away to chase a butterfly. When he happened to fall asleep, I wakened him, lest he should miss something I wished him to see. We spoke of the Father often and rapidly. I poured into his ears all the stories he ought to know, but we were often interrupted by the wind blowing, of which we must speak; by the coming out of the stars, which we must study; by the gurgling brook, which we must trace to its source.

Then in the twilight, we met the Father. The child merely glanced at him. The Father stretched out his hand, but the child was not interested enough to take it. Feverish spots burned on his cheeks. Exhausted, he dropped to the ground and fell asleep. Again I was between the child and the Father. I wondered. I had taught him so many, many things.

*   *   *   *

I took a little child's hand in mine. I was to lead him to the Father. My heart was full of gratitude for the glad privilege. We walked slowly. I suited my steps to the short steps of the child. We spoke of things the child noticed.

Sometimes it was one of the Father's birds; we watched it build a nest, and we saw the eggs that were laid. We wondered later at the care it gave its young.

Sometimes we picked the Father's flowers, stroked their soft petals, and loved their bright colors. Often we told stories of the Father. I told them to the child, and the child told them to me. We told them, the child and I, over and over. Sometimes we stopped to rest, leaning against the Father's trees, letting his air cool our brows, and never speaking.

Then in the twilight, we met the Father. The child's eyes shone. He looked up lovingly, trustingly, eagerly, into the Father's face; he put his hand into the Father's hand. For the moment I was forgotten. But I was content.[7]

For Discussion and Sharing

1. Share illustrations of the child's sensing of emotions and attitudes in your family.

2. What is bound to happen in the child's life when the parents profess one thing but practice another?

3. Can the child develop faith from informal example alone?

4. In which parable do we find ourselves living most of the time?

Making Family Life Spiritual

A child cannot be a whole person if only the physical, social, mental, and emotional needs are met but the spiritual need is ignored or left to develop on its own.

The child's spiritual life springs spontaneously from everyday life—the joys, delights, discoveries, questions, secret desires, good intentions, and events of family life. When under the stress of some emotion or event, the child experiences a vague longing and sensitivity of spirit. We should learn just what to say to reveal to the child the One for whom the human spirit secretly yearns. In this way God will become the object of the child's joys, desires, and the whole of life.

A persistent danger is that parents, particularly during early parenting years, may fail to nurture their own spiritual lives. This can bring disastrous results.
—John M. Drescher

5

Teachable Moments

A friend expressed their family goal this way: "We try to catch moments of beauty whenever they come or wherever they are and relate them to God and his plan for the total universe. Many times the children's concerns and interests lead to the threshold of worship."

She gives this example. "Our fifth grader, Billy, brought home his *Weekly Reader* so his mother and dad could 'learn about whales too.' Supper talk was a mixture of football and whales, . . . and God saw that it was good."

"You see, Billy," said his father, "even whales are a part of God's great plan."

Many times I am struck by the spontaneous expressions of a child on God's creation. At every turn a child can see God's handiwork. A stroll by a stream or through the park poses new opportunities of learning, both natural and spiritual. Parents remember questions such as these: "Daddy, how do the stars stay up in the sky? What makes some stones round and other stones sharp? How did God make the mountains so high?" These are excellent launching pads for conversation about God's greatness and glory.

What should parents do when the spontaneous questions and experiences of children lead to holy ground? Long ago Job was told to stand still and think of the wonders of God (Job 38—42). Too often parents pass by these opportunities rather than taking time to ponder with their children the wonders of God's creation and daily providence.

Few moments of family life are better for adding spiritual dimension than birthdays. These are milestones in the mind of a child. Birthdays can also be spiritual milestones in life pilgrimages. Then the emphasis can be on belonging and sharing and the recognition that we belong, not by giving gifts, but by sharing ourselves. Some children receive large gifts and yet feel unappreciated or rejected.

Consider the case of one child whose family provided a large cake, many new clothes and toys, and a substantial gift of money. But still the child felt neglected by his parents. He had no sense of really belonging. As he recalls, he seemed to sense inside that his parents were giving him things to avoid giving themselves.

Another young man speaks about the way his family celebrated his birthday when he was a child. They were too poor to purchase gifts. Yet his mother made a cake and used the candles kept from former birthdays.

From the love she expressed, he gained a deep sense of belonging. He felt worth and well-being because the family shared in making every birthday a great day. They commented on their young boy and his brother growing older and taller each year.

"I also remember," he says, "how my father prayed at the birthday meal. I knew my family and God in heaven were interested in me, and I belonged to all of them."

How easy it is for a child to build on the experience of belonging to such a family and thus to grow to understand belonging to God's family.

Pausing for prayer before leaving for church on Sunday morning makes churchgoing more than a routine or meaningless ritual. It is good for us to pray for those who minister and teach, asking God for a fresh insight of his will. Such things do not go unrewarded in building love for God, his church, and his word.

A beloved pastor in his nineties had many ways of making moments in the home deeply spiritual. One example was the blessing he gave departing guests.

When a family left his doorstep, they always walked away with a fresh God-consciousness. His daughter, now a college professor, wrote words of gratitude when reflecting on her home experience. When family and friends paused before farewells, her father asked them to join in a Scripture, song, or prayer together.

"Often," she said, "if the guests were traveling from a distance, we recited or sung the travelers' psalm:

As I journey through the land, singing as I go,
Pointing souls to Calvary, to the crimson flow,
Many arrows pierce my soul, from without, within
But my Lord leads me on, through him I must win.

Oh, I want to see him, look upon his face,
There to sing forever of his saving grace;
On the streets of glory, let me lift my voice,
Cares all past, home at last, ever to rejoice.[8]

"The words of the song, "elect from every nation, yet one o'er all the earth," [9] took on meaning as we prayed together in our Ohio parsonage with friends new and old, from east, west, north, south, and lands abroad," the daughter reported.

Another person remembers how his childhood family began each major trip. They would pause in the car and pray for God's care and protection on the journey.

Alan Loy McGinnis tells how his father did his teaching. "Looking back upon the dinner conversations with which I grew up, I now see how effectively my father used heroes to motivate his sons. A thoughtful, soft-spoken man, it would never enter into his mind to lecture us about excelling or studying hard in school. But at the dinner table, he did comment upon the people in our small town whom he admired—a businessman who was going to law school at night, or a young farmer who was taking correspondence classes. He wanted to be sure we noticed these people.

"Both my brother and I went on to get doctoral degrees and, looking back, I now see how strongly our father propelled us toward success. He did what all effective managers and teachers do—he gave us strong values by holding up flesh-and-blood people who embody these values." [10]

A fine book by Johann Christoph Arnold, *A Little Child Shall Lead Them*, has many solid Christian insights. Arnold talks of making sure we are leading our children to Jesus, not merely to religious traditions. " 'Let the children come to me,' says Jesus, not to your pious customs, your Christian traditions, but 'to me.' "

Arnold further writes,

> Along with reverence and love to God, teach your children gratefulness. Whether through grace at mealtimes or prayer at bedtime, urge them to thank God for all they have—for parents and family, friends, a roof over their head, clothes, food, and safety. Remind them, too, that not all children have what they have, and open their eyes to the needs of others. Assure them that God is their Father and that he is accessible to each of us, whether old or young.

Finally, teach your children by reading to them from the Bible. As they grow older, encourage them to learn important passages by heart, and point out how this or that verse can provide a rock on which to stand later in life, especially during difficult times. Remember though, that ultimately it is not memorized verses that will capture a child's heart, but the living example of adults who show love and respect for God and for each other in their deeds as well as their words. And never forget that children are often already much closer than we are to God. [11]

6

Our Fun and Our Faith

As an editor of a weekly magazine during our children's growing-up years, my work required me to be gone from home half the time. Sometimes a trip was as long as fifteen days.

Now my children are adults. At a recent parent-child retreat, a father looked at me squarely and said, "I want to know how your children feel about your being away from home so much of the time when they were young."

I replied, "The next time I visit my children, I'll ask each one that question."

I did ask that question. One of my surprises was that one after the other referred to the good times we had on many trips of camping across the country.

We stashed the old tent in the Ford when traveling to summer appointments. We would start early in the morning with the promise of stopping by early afternoon where the children could go swimming and we could spend the rest of the day enjoying ourselves as a family. These were high points. They were also spiritual experiences, as we worshiped, prayed, and sang along the way. The children also reminded me of my constant comment, "Now, children, look at that beautiful view." God's beautiful views became a point of humor.

I've also shared many times that my job and my children's happiness would have been an impossibility except for Betty, my wife. Each time, uncomplainingly, she had the children excited about my homecoming.

In a day of much family camping and travel, how can our families make these experiences deeply spiritual? Such occasions afford some of the easiest opportunities to call attention to God's creation.

One young man reflected on such an experience: "Some of my highest spiritual moments have been at family devotions in family camping."

Who has not felt spiritually strengthened while standing under the starry sky or sitting by a campfire, surrounded by God's handiwork?

One family took the Bible with them on vacation. When travel grew tiresome, the mother reached for the Bible and turned to Psalm 121. "I will lift up my eyes to the hills," she read. The family repeated after her, "I will lift up my eyes to the hills."

Through Psalm 121 and the family's repetition of it, the children received a valuable impression. As they reached the majestic Rockies, ten-year-old Anne remarked, "I'm glad we learned those verses about the hills, Mother, for today."

One day two of our children came home from a school field trip and told us the children on the bus sang nearly all the time. This was not new for our children, for we sang many favorite songs as we traveled. Sometimes we tried new ones. Singing is a good release for restless children. It refreshes all who join and adds spiritual dimension to the journey.

In a family of adolescent boys, the oldest had just passed his examination for a driver's license. He came home pleased, excited, and full of details about the experience. The conversation during supper included recounting the events, the advice he received, the hazards to be avoided, what was lawful, and what was not.

Father, appreciating the importance of the time, not only for the son but for all the family, suggested a family prayer. They would commit to God this family member who was assuming responsibility crucial to himself and countless others.

Two years later, the second son passed his examination for a driver's license. After supper he put his arm around his father's shoulder and asked, "How about a family prayer for me tonight, Dad? I think I need it as much as Arthur."

When some friends of ours built a new house, they found ways to give spiritual significance to the undertaking. As a family, they sought God's guidance before building. When they moved in, they planned a special service of dedication. They invited their pastor's family plus several close friends to share with them. They dedicated their home to God, promised to keep their home the kind of place in which Christ felt welcome, and committed themselves to offer friends and strangers a refuge of love.

7

For Special Strength

A young person serving in one of the world's trouble spots was asked by a friend, "How is it possible for you to stick it out in such a situation? Aren't the temptations terrific?"

"Yes," he answered, "the temptations are tremendous. But I can still hear my father and mother's prayer when I was ready to leave home. They asked God to keep me from wrong and to help me be faithful to him and to the teaching they sought to give me. I know my family is fervently praying for me as I serve here."

When young people go away to school or service, it is a great moment in family life. If our homes are to be spiritual launching platforms from which we send our children to serve the world, these moments of launching should carry a spiritual impact. If we share some guiding words from Scripture and pause for prayer by the gathered family at such a time, that will make an unforgettable experience.

Exchanging marriage vows creates a moment of spiritual significance. It should be joyous. Too often even Christian young people can recall their wedding only as a day of frills, food, and foolish stunts. We as Christian parents are challenged to add spiritual dimension. It is not so much a time to preach to those getting married as a time to teach younger children and remind everyone of the meaning of marriage. It is a time for parents to share with children their own love for each other and how God led them together.

"I remember when my cousin was married," said a happily married young wife. "On the way home from the wedding, my parents shared the joy they experienced when they were married. When they told us that their love for each other and their happiness now was greater than ever, I felt a sense of well-being that has given me stability many times since. That experience has cast a light across my entire life."

Even the death of a friend or of one in the family can be a moment of a growing spiritually. Such an event gives parents an opportunity to instill confidence in God in a deep way. In the time of separation and what seems the end, the child can be taught by the spirit, attitude, and words of adult believers. Parents can show their children how to be firmly based on those things which are eternal.

For the Christian, death is an opportunity to share deeply in sorrow and to show that faith in God frees us from fatalism and hopelessness. Even in the face of death, a family's faith can flower forth.

My parents took all of us children to the funerals of

relatives and friends. The way my father and mother shed tears of sorrow and sympathy, the words of hope they spoke to the bereaved, and the Christian message preached on such occasions—these all have helped give me a blessed and living hope.

The Andrew family took their two small sons to the funeral of a great-uncle the boys knew well. "We expected to be faced with many questions, and we were," said Mrs. Andrew. "But the fact that death represented no fear for them was what amazed me. Eight-year-old James talked calmly about death and seeing God. Four-year-old John wondered why he must wait to be older to die. We were happy to have assurance of life with God that goes beyond death, so we could lead them in thinking of life, death, and heaven."

8

Our Worship and Our Witness

"This morning I saw a beautiful picture," said a friend of mine as we met before a meeting. We were staying in different homes during a conference held in a college community.

He described the scene he saw when he came down for breakfast. Around the table was the entire family—the college chemistry professor, his spouse, and their five children. The children, ranging in age from five to late teens, had Bibles and songbooks. After singing several songs, they took turns reading the Scripture and praying. This family started the day with spiritual strength.

Family worship need not be only a thing of the past. For years many received a God-consciousness around the family altar which today's family might well cherish.

Through family worship children can learn their

relation to the larger family of God. In the family circle they can pray for the church, its ministers, and its worldwide mission. Thus their love and loyalty for Christ and the church will grow. As children's interests and friendships broaden, they learn to include people outside the in-group of family and close friends. Eventually family prayers can broaden so that children become missionary-minded in the basic sense of having concern for all people.

Bobby, who was in nursery school, thought of his father's house-to-house sales contacts. He included his father's customers in his prayer and asked God, "Please bless all the folks I don't know."

Many times I am amazed at the deep concern children have for others. After sharing someone's need, I have heard small children, on their own, remember that person in prayer day after day. When we hear about physical and spiritual needs and war and peace on the daily news, we have opportunities to clothe such with spiritual meaning and purpose.

In Deuteronomy 6:6-7, Moses tells us that the task of teaching and using available moments to teach is not to be a hit-and-run method. "Keep these words that I am commanding you today in your heart. Recite them to your children and talk about them when you are at home and when you are away, when you lie down and when you rise."

From one point of view, it is easy to mold children; children are impressionable. They are easily persuaded of the truth of what their parents teach them.

On the other hand, it is a tremendous undertaking to give children genuine Christian nurture and training. It is much easier for parents to neglect than to nurture their children for God. That is the reason for the steady emphasis of the Scriptures that parents speak of God and his works under all circumstances. When sitting in one's house, when walking in the way, when retiring for the night, when arising, whether relaxing at home or hurrying along a hot and dusty road—always the conversation shall turn to God and his Word.

To talk about God when retiring, arising, sitting, or walking means that our faith will be so meaningful to us that it will be natural in all circumstances of life to speak of God and his works. Notice that God says, "These words which I command you this day shall be upon your heart."

Parents have precious opportunities to relate all life to God. But opportunities are passing things. They must be seized immediately or be lost. We are called to make the most of every opportunity for God in the only family we will have. We are called to make our families demonstration centers of Christian living.

Henry Drummond wrote, "The family circle is the supreme conductor of Christianity." We must therefore hallow the daily duties and delights of family living with the touch of the divine.

For Discussion and Sharing

1. Where have you found teachable moments with your children?

2. In your perception, do your children think of your faith as being fun, full of joy, and something they associate with happiness?

3. In what other ways and situations can our children sense that God gives us special strength?

4. Does Deuteronomy 6:6-7 overwhelm you? Or does it challenge you to use the opportunities of each day and experience?

Portals
for Prayer

No doubt the place, practice, and naturalness of prayer in the family, more than any other thing, reveals the spiritual tone and heartbeat of the home. The adage remains true: "The family that prays together stays together."

Jesus said, "Where two or three are gathered in my name, I am present there." Think of the implications of that for the Christian family. Jesus also promised that "if two of you shall agree on anything in my name I will do it." That again brings it down to the family that prays.
—John M. Drescher

Family prayer is the key to the day and the lock of the night.
—Thomas Fuller

9

Parents and Prayer

In the 1960s the Supreme Court ruled against prescribed Bible reading and prayer in public schools. John F. Kennedy, then president, expressed hope that parents would make a renewed effort to teach their children at home.

That was a good and needed word. *Primary* responsibility for teaching the Scripture and for prayer cannot be pushed onto the school or even the church. The primary and basic nursery of the spiritual life is in the home. God intends the home to be the place where persons first learn to revere and love God.

It is impossible to think of a faithful Christian family without Scripture reading. Likewise, it is impossible to think of a vital spiritual home without prayer.

Too seldom do we stress the uniting, binding effect of prayer, particularly in the family. The old proverb that says, "The family that prays together stays together," is literally true. This is why I ask Christian young couples, when I counsel them for marriage, to make a covenant of prayer. I ask them to promise each other that they will pray together.

We assume that because couples are Christian, they will pray together. This is usually not true. Studies suggest that what couples discuss and agree on before marriage, they are more likely to follow after marriage. What they do not discuss and agree on before marriage, they rarely pursue after marriage.

Statistics show that in North America the divorce rate is approaching one in two marriages. For couples married in the church and attending church regularly, the divorce rate has dropped to one in fifty marriages. But in those marriages where husband and wife pray together, the divorce rate is only one in over a thousand marriages, claimed the *Chicago Catholic* recently. We might say there is nothing which holds a marriage together like praying with and for each other.

In speaking of prayer in the home, we must begin with parents. The atmosphere created by mother and father will show what is important in their life. Prayer will have meaning as the parents give it meaning.

Like nearly everything the child learns early in life, prayer is caught more than taught. The child is sensitive to moods, attitudes, and expressions of all kinds. The child is quick to pick up what is important to parents, whether positive or negative. This means parents need to pray if their children are to pray, join in family prayer, and look to God.

There are more formal times for prayer at meals, bedtimes, and rituals of family worship. However, the most effective examples of prayer often take place in the informal, ordinary happenings of every family. If prayer centers only on the formal, the child begins to divide life into secular and sacred. Rather than encourage this division, we need to emphasize that all of life is sacred. Any place can be a worship setting. We can come to God in prayer at any time.

Our daughter Sandy and son-in-law John, and their children, Maria (six) and Jonathan (two), were seated on the floor before the fireplace. They had moved into the modest yet adequate house only a short time before. As they sat there with the lights off, in the glow of the fireplace, they spoke of God's goodness in leading them to this house. They noted how wonderful it was to have a fireplace to gather around.

Maria asked, "Could we call this a miracle?"

That comment by a kindergarten girl led to a discussion of God's acts and to a prayer of thanksgiving by a little family that evening.

Parents often overlook opportunities to weave prayer into the fabric of family life. A friend said, "We try to catch moments of beauty whenever they come, wherever they are, and relate them to God and the created universe. Many times our children's concerns and interests lead us to the threshold of worship."

Children are also quick to sense needs of those around them. The young child can have deep concern for others. Mention some person or need in prayer, and a small child will remember it for days to come.

When we foster prayer in family settings, we develop active and engaged spirituality. Such dedication to God reaches into all of life now and in the future.

10

Obstacles and Opportunities

Discussions of family worship, prayer, and time together produce varied excuses: "We have so little time. We lack an ideal place. In the morning everyone is too rushed; in the evening we're too tired. Everyone has a different schedule. We don't always feel like praying and can't always get in the mood for it." Some also share honestly, "We feel like the early disciples when they said, 'Lord, teach us to pray'" (Luke 11:1).

These can be hurdles to prayer, but we must start by confessing the biggest obstacle. We lack commitment to prayer. Otherwise, we would make time for it.

When a family commits itself to pray, whether daily or weekly, possibilities are great. Prayer can then be woven into life as fully as commitments to play sports, practice music, or shop for groceries.

Certain aids to prayer are good to keep in mind. There are times when we will proceed with prayer even though not every member of the family is around. We are wise to make prayer a family experience at a time most convenient to all. Yet we need not be discouraged or dissuaded if sometimes not all can be present.

Plan for prayer when there is the least time pressure. This may be difficult. But it is most helpful to share needs, concerns, and spend time in prayer when people do not feel rushed.

Unless a regular time is planned, the prayer time will likely be omitted. It is better occasionally to miss a regular time than not to have a set time and through such negligence let family worship and prayer disappear.

Meaningful prayer time takes planning. Someone should see that there *is* a plan and that family members know of the time and place. Some families post a reminder at a prominent place. They may also have a sheet on which family members can write prayer requests for family prayer time.

Variety is particularly important for young children. Prayer time should include each member of the family, regardless of age. All should have the opportunity to participate in sharing and praying.

Here are a few suggestions to help your family pray together.

- Schedule family prayer time in connection with family meals, when as many family members as possible can be present. Make this an opportunity for family members to pray about things that have happened during the day.
- Begin your time of prayer by lighting a family can-

dle or individual candles for each family member. Children especially appreciate this.

- You may wish to choose a weekly prayer emphasis. This theme can center on needs of family members, friends, relatives, neighbors, or on the seasons of Thanksgiving, Advent, Christmas, Lent, Easter, and so on.
- Spend time together reading from the Psalms, the Gospels, the letters of Paul, and other religious texts.
- Discuss different kinds of prayer, such as prayers of praise, thanksgiving, intercession, confession, petition, and dedication.
- Once a week or on some special occasion, invite one or more family members to write an original prayer and use it to lead the family in prayer.
- Many great church hymns are also prayers. Sing a prayer song, then ponder the words in silence.
- Always take time to invite each family member to share something personal from the day, about which the family can pray or join in giving thanks to God.
- Use gestures such as opening one's hands to receive from the Lord, raising hands in praise to God, and joining hands to pray with each other. These can be especially meaningful ways to add symbolic action to your prayer experience together.[12]

The family that prays together stays together; such a family also knows and experiences some of the greatest joys possible in this life, including love, happiness, peace, and oneness.

11

Catching Thankfulness

When our son Ron was three, he said he wanted to ask the blessing on the meal. We gladly agreed. He began with thanking God for specific things he saw as he peeped with partially bowed head. He prayed, "I thank you, God, for our plates; I thank you for our forks; I thank you for our knives; I thank you for our water; I thank you for our bread."

On and on he kept going as he moved from things on the table to things around the room. Even Betty's and my patience was tried as he prayed his marathon prayer.

Afterward, I pondered that prayer many times. Our son is now the father of two boys and two girls, the oldest in college. Though I can't remember him ever praying such a lengthy prayer again, he has always had a thankful spirit.

Our friend Cheryl shared her two-and-a-half-year-old son's Christmas prayer. "We read the story of Jesus' birth. Each of us prayed a prayer of thanks, beginning with Jordan. His hands were folded piously, but his eyes looked around the room as he prayed, 'Thank you for the Christmas tree, thank you for the lights, thank you for our presents, thank you for the angels, thank you for the Christmas tree, and thank you for underwear. Amen.'

"He missed Jesus and zeroed in on the Christmas tree twice. But he thanked God for something I had never thanked God for—underwear!"[13]

As Christian parents, we want our children to be thankful. Their spirit of gratitude has much to do with a happy life and relationships. Parents cannot start too early encouraging a thankful attitude. The first years of life may well be the most opportune time to develop a thankful disposition and outlook. But how is it done?

A thankful spirit is caught more than taught. Gratitude is an attitude. We know that, just as children are sensitive to our moods, attitudes, and expressions, they are quick to pick up parents' attitudes of thanksgiving. Witness how early the child loves to join in prayer around the table. As children feel and hear a spirit of gratitude, they automatically pick up that outlook.

We tell children to say "Thank you" or "Please" when asking for something or receiving it. What we desire even more is for our children to respond in this way without being told.

Each of us has known parents who are free to express sincere thanks to others as well as to each other in the family. When this is true, it is almost certain that the child from such a family will also be free to express thanks.

Our four-year-old grandson is such a child. It is not unusual for him to stop in the middle of his meal, as well as at the end, to say, "Thank you, Mommy (or Grandma), for the good food."

Such an expression warms the hearts of all. Where did he get this idea? I think I know. His parents are quick to express thanks to each other and to others.

12

Where Thankfulness Begins

One evening I was watching a church league ball game. A young mother shared with me that her father asked her three-year-old, "Where did you get your curly, blonde hair?" Grandfather thought the child would say that he got it from his father, who had a full head of blonde, curly hair.

However, to the surprise of all, he replied, "I got it from God."

Where did he get the idea that God is his Creator and that God should get the credit?

A thankful spirit or attitude begins with a consciousness of God's goodness and blessing. Thankfulness is a recognition of God. The Scripture suggests a mark of those who are on the road away from God: "They did not honor him as God or give thanks to him" (Rom. 1:21).

When we live thankful lives, we train our children

to live thankful and God-honoring lives rather than having a complaining spirit. In addition, we teach our children to keep their eyes on God and the good things in life, conscious of the blessings God gives.

In our family, as in many Christian families, the use of Christian songs of thanksgiving is an important element. Songs were a regular part of our worship when the children were small. One still rings in my ears, and I now hear grandchildren sing it when I visit them:

> Thank you for the world so sweet,
> Thank you for the food we eat,
> Thank you for the birds that sing,
> Thank you, God, for everything." [14]

Parents who freely share stories of God's goodness and blessing create a spirit of thanksgiving.

Family prayers have much to do with building praise and gratitude. Even greater is a spontaneous prayer when we receive good news, when we have special needs supplied, or when we experience God's protection and provision throughout the day.

Take time at meals or in family worship to share what each person is thankful for and to pray with thanksgiving for blessings mentioned. This is something the small child can participate in and enjoy.

Thank God for a safe trip home, for what God has provided after a shopping trip, for the Sunday services at church, for a warm home, for clothes to wear. These are simple yet meaningful ways of developing a thankful spirit.

Another important way we teach our children the spirit of thankfulness is by expressing appreciation and thanks for other people. Parents project a natural and powerful example of a thankful spirit when they pray for and thank God for teachers, the church, schools, pastors, other church workers, for neighbors, and playmates.

We have been blessed through entertaining many guests flowing through our home over the years. Our children learned to know and appreciate people from different races, cultures, and vocations. They developed friendships with people from around the world.

As we provided a home for people with disabilities and people with varying needs, God gave us an added sense of appreciation for his gifts of people, different abilities, and the blessings of life. This has yielded a spirit of appreciation and thanksgiving for the health, strength, and blessings we daily receive.

Giving is a wonderful way to fill our lives with thanksgiving. One cannot give without becoming more thankful—thankful to have something to give, thankful for the privilege of giving, thankful to know that giving is God's will, thankful to be part of God's program and action in our lives and in the world. There is no better way of being thankful than by sharing freely and being a blessing to others.

Children love to give. At times they have selfish streaks, but children often love the joy of sharing. They catch the spirit from parents who model giving, who encourage the child to share toys and gifts, and who lead the child even from an early age to place something in the offering at church.

Once our family was in church beside a young family. The baby, in the father's arms, was not yet one year old. The other two children were probably three and five. As the offering was taken, I noticed that each child—including the baby—had a coin. Each had a cheerful face while placing the money in the offering. In the child's earliest years, parents can teach the grace of giving and sharing.

Our ten-year-old granddaughter Ginger received pay for something she was asked to do. She quickly figured out the part she wanted to give in the church offering. "And look at all I have left," she said. Where did Ginger get the idea to give this portion to the Lord's work and to do it so cheerfully? The answer is easy. Her parents show that same spirit of generosity.

As parents we know that thanksgiving is an attitude that can be cultivated. Our children catch our attitudes even before they talk or walk. The mind-set of thankfulness is a basic outlook on the world under God's providential care. It opens us up to happiness, health, and blessings all through life.

For Discussion and Sharing

1. Do you agree that prayer, more than anything else, sets the spiritual tone of the home?

2. Share your own experience in family prayer, in your childhood family, and in your present family.

3. Talk about obstacles your family faces in praying together, reading the Bible, and family worship.

4. Discuss ways your family can develop a spirit of thanksgiving.

Celebrating Togetherness

From the home of my childhood I have brought nothing but precious memories, for there are no memories more precious than those of early childhood in one's first home. And that is almost always so if there is any love and harmony in the family at all. Indeed, precious memories may remain even of a bad home, if only the heart knows how to find what is precious. —Fyodor Dostoyevsky

Love is always spelled T—I—M—E. Time for togetherness, for sharing, for caring.

We remember few things in life which we did alone, unless they were bad things. The good things we remember are the things we did with others, particularly with family. —John M. Drescher

13

Togetherness—the Need and Message

In his youth, Brooks Adams, son of onetime ambassador to Great Britain Charles Francis Adams, wrote in his diary: "Went fishing with my father. The most glorious day of my life."

So happy was the memory of that day with his father that for thirty years thereafter he made repeated references to it in his diary.

However, the rest of the story is sad. Charles Francis Adams wrote in his diary, "Went fishing with my son. A day wasted."

Many times I have asked persons of all ages, at gatherings ranging from family retreats to seminars, to think back to their childhood. I have asked them to recall one or more good times that come immediately to mind which they still treasure.

Their response to such questions shows that the lasting experiences remembered from childhood are those shared with other family members. Even with effort, we can remember only a few good individual happenings. But we do remember family times together. Many times each of us has said, "I remember when . . ." Those memories are an important part of who we are.

Togetherness is spending time with one another. It's taking time to talk, to listen, to play with one another, to go places, to share life in a multitude of meaningful ways. Togetherness speaks of the experiences, both planned and unplanned, that build unity and a sense of love and appreciation for one another.

If we are to experience such times as families, we have to make a definite decision to plan togetherness. In the average family's schedule, members are going in different directions. If times to be together are not planned, families can experience loneliness, even estrangement, while living in the same house.

Even the family that plans special times together may overlook many moments that could be times of special closeness. Togetherness dare not wait only for special times. These may seem hollow if everyday experiences are not used for building the spirit of togetherness. It is better to use five minutes each day to talk, listen, and share than to wait for significant times once or twice a year.

Spending time together is the best way to say, "I love you, I like to be with you, you mean much to me." The gift of time from a loved one gives each of us a sense of significance, a feeling that we are appreciated, an inner sense of security and acceptance.

14

Those Special Times

In a family retreat, a woman who grew up in Switzerland described an experience from childhood. She told about difficult times. Families worked long, hard days. To keep bread on the table, the family shared the farmwork and had little time for recreation.

However, one day her mother took a half day to make a straw doll with her daughter. That doll became a cherished possession, not only because it was part of a little girl's daily play, but also because it was a remembrance of their half day together.

Each family has special times that are built-in opportunities to experience togetherness. Birthdays, which delight our children, can give the birthday child deep feelings of belonging, feelings basic to any child's emotional and mental well-being. Our children need the assurance that we value them as members of the inner circle. This feeling is far more important than any material gift, despite the temptation to substitute gifts for time together.

This principle carries through for all other important occasions, such as Christmas or special days at school and church. A sense of well-being grows from activities that show how we belong to the family or the group. Feelings of warmth and love flow from shared emotions, from the joys as well as the disappointments we experience.

A beloved great-grandfather remembered just such joy. His father had saddled up two horses for his son and himself. Together they rode over the mountain to a spot his father had selected, to gather chestnuts. As he spoke, his face reflected the joy of that experience. "I can still sense the love and satisfaction I felt when my father left his work to spend a whole day with me. I felt I was really important to him. But most of all, I felt love."

How often our children talk about a hike in the woods or a camping trip! These treasured times are remembered throughout life. Our children can recite in detail these good times—the prayers we prayed lying in our sleeping bags, the wailing winds tearing at the tent's edges, the rainstorms we braved as we snuggled in the tent to keep dry.

When we talk about what interests us and listen to the interests of others, we feel togetherness. Chatting around the family table can be such a time. Why have great writers centered so much drama on conversation at the table? Because eating together draws persons into a closeness that sitting in a living room does not provide. Happy is the home in which members linger around the table, sharing excitement and concerns.

Some families have what they call "sharing time," a period planned to allow their members to talk about the happenings of the day. When children are small, a family "show and tell" builds feelings of love and appreciation.

Some families find that sharing their financial situation brings the members closer. One family was concerned about a daughter who was careless in her use of hot water, electricity, and other resources. When the parents described how much it cost per person each month to keep the household going, she became eager to reduce unnecessary costs. Shared family projects hold families together. These may include making a garden, going to the woods to gather firewood, and driving to the forest to select the family Christmas tree.

We say, "Families that pray together stay together." We could add, "Families that play together stay together." Few things build a sense of togetherness better than parents and children enjoying vigorous, athletic games as well as indoor games, puzzles, and reading aloud.

From early childhood, parents should cultivate togetherness through play. One father who came home tired was playing with his small son. As they scrambled together on the floor, a friend walked in and asked, "Why do you do that when you are so tired?"

He replied, "I'd rather have a backache now than a heartache later."

Through play children develop a sense of togetherness and also learn fairness and cooperation from their parents.

15

Spiritual Sharing

Happy the home in which parents and children, from the start, know togetherness in religious practices and commitment. Many a child can point to this form of togetherness as basic in developing a solid foundation for all of life. Attending church together, praying together, and reading the Bible together give an inner strength that can be built in no other way.

No matter how strong or healthy otherwise, children suffer when the family lacks unity in religious life and practice. The spiritual dimension is essential.

One man, reflecting on his childhood, speaks for many persons. "We had many happy times together in our family. We played together, worked together, and hiked the woods together.

"Yet the times I felt closest to my parents and brothers and sisters were when we were together and prayed for one another. Then I sensed that a unity and a love existed between us which nothing could ever tear apart. We were together in joy and sorrow, and the God of heaven was with us."

The good times of togetherness are the experiences which linger longest in our memory. What we did alone is soon forgotten. The person rich in memories is wealthier by far than the multimillionaire who has sought meaning in money and things.

Dostoyevsky concludes his great novel *The Brothers Karamazov* with Alyosha pointing out the importance of good memories: "My dear children, perhaps you will not understand what I'm going to say to you now, for I often speak very incomprehensively, but I'm sure, you will remember that there's nothing higher, stronger, more wholesome and more useful in life than some good memory, especially when it goes back to the days of your childhood, to the days of your life at home.

"You are told a lot about your education, but some beautiful memory, preserved since childhood, is perhaps the best education of all. If a man carries many such memories into life with him, he is saved for the rest of his life. And even if only one good memory is left in our hearts, it may also be the instrument of our salvation one day."[15]

Pity the parents and children who think life can be complete without the spiritual dimension. Happy the family that recognizes the spiritual dimension of life is as necessary for wholeness and wellness as any other. Here is the greatest kind of togetherness.

16

Electronic Media— Curse or Blessing?

·I will walk with integrity of heart within my house;
I will not set before my eyes anything that is base. . . .
I will look with favor on the faithful of the land,
so that they may live with me. . . .
No one who practices deceit shall remain in my house;
no one who utters lies shall continue in my presence.
—Psalm 101:2, 6-7

In Psalm 101 the writer makes a fourfold covenant. The psalmist covenants to walk with integrity in his family. He says that only those who model faithfulness shall be invited into his house. He determines that all deceit and lying shall have no place in his home or presence.

What do such Scriptures say in a day when TV alone has the capacity to bring so much that is vile into our homes? When the canned laughter and humor center on deceit? When illicit behavior is not only portrayed but affirmed? When the average child sees eleven thousand murders by adolescence?

A psychologist friend said to me, "The sharpest and highest-paid psychologists of our time are not doing what I am doing. I am counseling persons who are dealing with personal, family, and social problems they face. The brightest psychologists are hired by corporations to tell them how to package and stack goods in stores so people will buy what they do not need."

This is only one aspect of the influence of the media in our time. We are bombarded all day and all night with sights and sounds. We are influenced by electronic media prepared by the most skilled communicators of our day. We absorb the messages which lead us to assume a lot of things with little or no thought. In fact, messages and values are so subtle and constant we may not even be aware of what is happening.

The choices we make powerfully determine what our children become. Nowhere is this more true than in our choices about the electronic media, including television, radio, computers, and the Internet.

What are Christian parents to make of these media? How much should we provide them for our children? Should our children watch television? What kind of programming? How much? How about movies? Should we buy them the toys and other merchandise that go with today's popular children's movies? Am I putting my child at a disadvantage as a citizen of tomorrow if I don't provide computer and Internet access? What about computer games? Radio or CD headset players? Do these choices matter?

Ron Helmuth, an expert in mass media, worked for fifteen years in data and information processing for one of America's largest corporations. He is now director of a university's information systems. Ron has kindly helped to develop the views of electronic media shared in this chapter and the next.

With Ron's help, I can declare that our choices about media do matter a great deal, though we seldom think about these questions! The electronic environment we provide for our children impacts their values and the way their minds work—in short, what they become.

The electronic environment influences our children in two ways. First, the content of these media powerfully shapes our children's values. This is a familiar argument. Of course, what our children see on TV and computer games affects them. It teaches them what is natural. The tens of thousand of hours that our children are engaged by the media powerfully teach that gratuitous violence and irresponsible sex are natural rather than deeds we should condemn, be alarmed by, or even avoid.

The second way electronic media determine what our children become is more subtle and far-reaching. We are mostly oblivious to it, so powerfully are we immersed in these changes ourselves. The media affect the child's ability to experience intimacy, settle disagreements, make sense of complexity, concentrate deeply, and have a rich inner thought life.

Some children use electronic devices nearly all their waking hours. They likely do so with our blessing. These media promise wonderful things—entertainment, education, inspiration, news, and information. What's more, they deliver on their promises.

They *do* entertain, educate, and inspire. But at what cost? With what effect? The changes in our children are deep and stay with them into adulthood. Children who heavily engage TV, computer games, and electronic media are changed persons. Such children have radically different abilities and interests than they would have if they had focused on other activities.

These changes happen whether the content of the programming is wholesome and Christian or unwholesome and destructive. The changes are caused by the media themselves and not just by the message or the content.

17

Electronic Media— Consequences and Changes

There are definite consequences apparent to those who have an understanding of the electronic media.

First, heavy use of electronics, especially television and some computer games, plays havoc with a child's attention span. These media jump abruptly from subject to subject and condition the child to quick changes of thought. It becomes harder for the child to concentrate on a task and finish it. After a few minutes, patience disappears.

The television industry itself would deny such criticism and demand to know what study proves that television impairs a child's attention span. But parents can see it for themselves. Watch how agitated and disquieted your child becomes after watching TV. The electronic child, one who experiences life electronically, is in danger of being easily distracted.

Second, heavy media usage hurts a child's social skills. Electronic life, whether in the form of computers, TV, headsets, or the Internet, replaces interaction with friends and family. Family life ends when electronics begin. Children develop skills by doing. When we choose electronics for our children, we give them fewer opportunities to be social.

Third, an electronic child lacks balance, because there's just not the time to do all the things a child needs to do to grow and still have time for many hours a day to be electronic. Use of electronic media reduces time for play, intimacy, exercise, contemplation, and being with friends.

Fourth, the electronic world teaches children a fragmented and shallow approach to reading. Electronically presented information (CD-ROMs, World Wide Web) tends to emphasize special effects and the ability to jump to related topics. Similarly, television tends to jump from scene to scene and also emphasizes special effects. The child immersed in this environment learns a different way of reading than the child absorbed in books.

Reading a book requires a certain stick-to-itiveness. To understand a book, one must start at the beginning and follow it through to the end, possibly reading hundreds of pages for many hours. When a new concept is presented, the child may need to stop and reflect on it. The child may even need to look back and reread for a missed or forgotten detail.

Such reading requires intense concentration and mental discipline. It is often called deep reading and contrasts starkly with the shallow mental habits a child learns by watching television, playing a computer game, or surfing the Internet.

Parents may replace the programming on secular TV with Christian TV or buy Christian computer games rather than non-Christian computer games. But that misses the point. The act of using electronic media is as much the problem as the content.

A precious gift parents can give the child is a non-electronic home. A home where the family talks, debates, and plays together without competing with the electronic world, where children must entertain themselves by playing creatively. A home where books are treasured, read, and discussed. A home where music is played on instruments and sung rather than merely listened to. A home where the TV and home computer are far from the family's daily living space of the den or the living room.

What will become of a child from such a home? This child will be focused and calm, have much social interaction each day, and engage in active pursuits rather than passively waiting for life to unfold. The child will be able to think and read deeply. This child will become a happier, more resourceful, and more highly skilled adult than a child immersed in our culture's electronic environment. Such children will not be at a disadvantage in the electronic information age but will have a distinct advantage. Concentration, resourcefulness, and understanding have never been more important than now.

If you decide your home will be a limited or non-electronic home, you will find yourself going against powerful popular currents. Friends will consider you quaint or eccentric. You'll receive no support from the electronic media itself, a multibillion-dollar industry that clamors for our attention. They powerfully proclaim that we should listen and engage. They promise great things.

As a parent, you choose the electronic environment you provide for your children. Your children will live with the consequences all their lives.

18

Let There Be Joy

François de Fenelon wrote many years ago, "If virtue offers itself to the child under melancholy and constraint, while liberty and license present themselves under an agreeable form, all is lost, and your labor is in vain."

On the other hand, if the good we seek to show the children is given in happy, joyful spirit, they will respond because the child is made for joy and should be surrounded by joy. It is important that life, and particularly religious life, be experienced in the atmosphere of joy.

Joy opens the child up to life. Then, far from being paralyzed and under constraint, the child spontaneously makes use of all potentialities. Christianity has lost its evangelistic and true nurturing ability when it appears joyless and unhappy. It is a sad day when parents lose the ability to have fun, to love, to play, and to enjoy life—particularly with their children.

A sage rightly said, "Never fear spoiling children by making them happy. Happiness is the atmosphere in which all good affections grow—the wholesome warmth necessary to make the heart blood circulate healthily and freely; unhappiness—the chilling pressure which produces here an inflammation, there an excrescence, and, most of all 'the mind's green and yellow sickness'—ill temper."[16]

Healthy children are happy children—most of the time. Children naturally take a marvelous delight in the world around them. They respond with intense interest and joy to the smallest discovery and events.

It is crucial for life to be experienced in an atmosphere of joy. Oscar Wilde wrote, "The best way to make children good is to make them happy." Charles Buxton said, "The first duty to children is to make them happy." We somehow know this is true. Our hearts sink when we see a sad and suffering child. God made children to be happy, to laugh, to enjoy life. The child should be surrounded by joy.

Blessed is that family in which joy abounds. Marion Kinneman writes, "Blessed are the fathers and mothers who have learned laughter; for it is the music of the child's world."

A warning: Some parents think they can produce a happy home by providing material things. If one parent doesn't make enough money, the other goes to work. Our society has perverted our perspective. We are being sold a bill of goods, the false theory that we owe our children all the things they want. Some even say, "We want our children to have all the things we never had." Then children have things but don't know who they are. Parents don't have time for the family. They think they can substitute things for themselves.

Material things are not the most important part of life. Things do not produce happiness. We must remind ourselves of this again and again.

Scripture remains clear: "Unless the Lord builds the house, those who build it labor in vain. . . . It is in vain that you rise up early and go late to rest, eating the bread of anxious toil; for he gives sleep to his beloved" (Ps. 127:1-2). The bread of sorrows is simply food secured through anxious and ceaseless striving for more.

With this needed warning, let us return to the call for joy and gladness in our homes. Walter Wangerin Jr. says it beautifully.

"Let the children laugh and be glad.

"O my dear, they haven't long before the world assaults them. Allow them genuine laughter now. Laugh *with them*, till tears run down your faces—till a memory of pure delight and precious relationship is established with them, indestructible, personal, and forever. . . .

"So give your children (your grandchildren, your nieces and nephews, the dear ones, children of your neighbors and your community)—give them golden days, their own pure days, in which they are so clearly and dearly loved that they believe in love and in their own particular worth when love shall soon be in short supply hereafter. Give them laughter."[17]

For Discussion and Sharing

1. Do you agree that we remember few things we did alone, but the good things we all remember are those we did with other persons?

2. Discuss the idea that love is spelled T—I—M—E.

3. What built-in opportunities does your family have for togetherness?

4. What are the good memories you have from your childhood?

5. Do you agree with Ron Helmuth's statements about the effects of the electronic media on our lives? What can the Christian family do in seeking a Christian approach or response?

6. Read Psalm 101:1-7. Discuss the implication of these verses in relation to mass media. Read and discuss Philippians 4:8-9.

Let Us
Take Heart

*God never expected parents to be perfect. As in the beauty of
the biblical account, God gives us the raw materials of life.
Parenting becomes a living laboratory for
experiencing divine grace and love.*

*The well-adjusted child does not come from the home which
made the fewest mistakes. The happy child comes from the
home which made many mistakes but love came through.
Forgiveness flourished,
and the door of the heart remained open.*

*Train children in the right way; and when old, they will not
stray* (Prov. 22:6). *This verse does not mean that if we as
parents do everything right, the child will have no choice.
God does everything right with us, yet we can also choose
against God and his commandments.* —John M. Drescher

*All your children shall be taught by the Lord, and
great shall be the prosperity of your children.* —Isaiah 54:13

19

The Weight of Parenting

When we think of the awesome responsibilities of parenting, we may be frightened by the weight of duty. God has entrusted to parents this rising generation. Will we be able to do our part, so that the Lord will "find faith on earth" when he returns? (Luke 18:8).

We can learn from the story of Moses. In the wilderness Moses was busy from morning till night, acting as a judge in the people's disputes. His father-in-law told him, "You will surely wear yourself out. . . . For the task is too heavy for you; you cannot do it alone" (Exod. 18:18).

We need to recognize that the task of parenting is too heavy for us alone. We have the Lord's help, the resources of Scripture and a heritage of faith, and a church community with experienced parents. These friends can give us wise counsel and provide us with wider perspective when we feel overwhelmed. There are also professional family counselors who can help us.

No doubt we parents will make mistakes and sometimes fail our children. We may only partly live up to God's charge to us to nurture, correct, and encourage our children. We may feel so rushed in the hectic pace of modern life that we neglect to stay close to our children.

Let us examine our lives and always trust the Lord to forgive us and give us opportunity and strength to overcome our mistakes. If God's love is truly in us, we will find a way to show that love first to those in our own families. And God can use that love to cover a multitude of sins or failings (1 Pet. 4:8).

Parents need to maintain their proper role as leaders in the family, those who guide, set limits, and light the way by raising the torch of faith. Yet one way we can help to share the faith is by confessing parental failings to our children. This will show them that we are human, and that we care for them even though we are not perfect. It will also demonstrate how we parents—and thus our children, too—can repent, turn, and be healed in family relationships.

Thus we can take important steps in becoming trustworthy companions and leaders of our children. May God grant us grace to live the faith with those closest to us.

20

But God . . .

Perhaps you saw the cartoon of the child cowering under the glare of a father, who caught the child in an act of disobedience. The child looks up and asks, "Dad, would you say this is because of heredity or environment?"

As parents, many times we are not sure ourselves what causes our children to become the persons they are. Many factors and forces are involved. We know there is good guidance from the Scriptures, the enrichment and encouragement of other persons, and the presence of God. So let us be encouraged.

Was there ever a time in history when it was easy to rear a family? Probably not. If you had to choose a time to live and to have a family, what time would you select? The early days of Christianity, when immorality was rampant? The Middle Ages, when the lamp of faith had nearly flickered out? More recent times and places where nations and laws at times work against the family?

At no time in history has the family had so many resources for being Christian. Often the only thing lacking today is the commitment to follow Christ daily. We shrink from practicing what we already know, from using the abundant resources of people, books, and programs designed to make our family strong, stable, and a spiritual bulwark for God.

Being a happy Christian family is not easy. There are no quick solutions or plans. Pressures are great. But there is also much encouragement. The family, the first institution created by God, is not without his help.

Remember the story of Noah recorded in Genesis 6-9. Great inspiration for each family can be found here. During days of great moral decay, Noah instilled in his children respect for the moral law of God. When other families turned from God, godliness, and goodness, Noah's family had firm faith. Learning from his example, his children stood true in the face of ridicule and rebellion against God and all that was good.

One can imagine Noah's children saying, "But, Dad, no one else is building an ark. Everyone else does as they please. We're the only family who lives like this. Why must we make fools of ourselves?"

Noah's family alone loved God and worshiped God (Heb. 11:7). His family alone paid attention to God's commands. Noah placed God and his worship first in their home.

Through his firm faith and calm, confident commitment to God, Noah convinced his family and saw the salvation of all of them (1 Pet. 3:20).

What a challenge! How could Noah do it? Was there ever such an example of a God-honoring family? This shows that a believing family can withstand ridicule and accomplish a lot.

Today our situation is different. Most of us are surrounded with at least some others who love God.

Yet Noah was not perfect; after the flood his children found him drunk. But perhaps this too is a source of encouragement. Despite our flaws, we parents can nurture godly families.

A child learns and grows by experience, example, and precept. We cannot disassociate these three. We cannot tell which is the most important at any given moment because they are so entwined from birth. Because of this, parents need to be persons who seek to live with proper emotions and attitudes, to live as examples of what they want their children to be, and to teach faithfully day by day.

New habits, ideas, and beliefs are not completely learned until they are part of the child's own experience. But have we also come to understand something of the tremendous power of example and of the right word at the right time. These help the child understand and evaluate experience.

True values of life must also be maintained. As one writer says, we no longer care to use oil lamps but always want to hold onto the torch of truth. We no longer install the old kitchen hand pump for water but always want to have the water of life.

We don't want to return to the old wood furnace but do need the faith of our fathers and mothers which carried them through difficult days. We do not want to return to plowing with a horse. But we still need that love for the Savior which also leads us to love one another. Faith, love, truth, and hope are never out of date.

In the first chapter of the New Testament, we have a list of persons. Some wicked ones had godly parents. Some godly persons had parents who failed miserably.

Let us draw cheer from knowledge that human beings can change and grow in spite of a bad heritage or an unfortunate environment. Yes, these do make the task more difficult. But even if both heritage and environment are negative, there is still the possibility of changing the way we look at them and the uses we make of them. As Christians, certainly of all people, we believe God can help us make positive changes. We are not helpless and hopeless.

Nurture, education, growth—these are the tasks. Each parent's privilege is to fulfill these tasks by bringing a family to love and reverence God. Each family's challenge is to pass on the torch of faith.

For Discussion and Sharing

1. How do you see parenting? As a weight, struggle, privilege, joy?

2. Do you think it is more difficult to rear a family today than in the past? In what ways?

3. What are the abiding values, as you see them?

Notes

1. Ross Campbell, *How to Really Love Your Child* (Wheaton, Ill.: Victor Books, 1982), 129.

2. F. W. Richardson, *Parenthood and the Newer Psychology* (Darby, Pa.: Arden Library, 1979 reprint of 1926 ed.).

3. Ralph Heynen, *The Secret of Christian Family Living* (Grand Rapids: Baker Book House, 1965), 48.

4. One paragraph recast from John M. Drescher, *Seven Things Children Need* (Scottdale, Pa.: Herald Press, 1988), 118.

5. Three paragraphs recast from John M. Drescher, *If I Were Starting My Family.Again* (Intercourse, Pa.: Good Books, 1994), 54-55.

6. Evelyn Ruth Mills Duvall, *Faith in Families* (Chicago, Ill.: Rand McNally and Co., 1970), 24.

7. Adapted from an unknown author.

8. Source unknown.

9. Samuel J. Stone, in his hymn "The Church's One Foundation" (1865).

10. Alan Loy McGuinnis, *Bringing Out the Best in People* (Minneapolis: Augsburg Press, 1985), 97.
11. Johann Christoph Arnold, *A Little Child Shall Lead Them* (Farmington, Pa.: Plough Publishing, 1997), 61-62.
12. Adapted from John M. Drescher, *Bringing Your Family Together in Prayer* (St. Meinrad, Ind.: Abbey Press, 1993), 3.
13. Drescher, *Bringing Your Family Together in Prayer*, 5.
14. Jonathan Battishill, from *Father, Hear Thy Children Sing*, copyright © 1953, by Hall and McCreary Co.
15. Fyodor Dostoyevsky, *The Brothers Karamazov* (New York: Penguin, 1982), 910-911.
16. Quoted in Drescher, *If I Were Starting My Family Again*, 20-21.
17. Walter Wangerin Jr., *Little Lamb, Who Made Thee?* (Grand Rapids: Zondervan, 1993.

The Author

John M. Drescher, Harrisonburg, Virginia, has served as a pastor, editor, counselor, seminary teacher, and writer.

Drescher has authored thirty-seven books. More than a dozen relate to husband-and-wife as well as parent-and-child relationships. *Seven Things Children Need* is now printed in fourteen languages. *If I Were Starting My Family Again* was condensed in *Readers Digest*.

Other books by Drescher include *When Your Child Is 6 to 12, Meditations for the Newly Married, Doing What Comes Spiritually, If I Were Starting My Ministry Again, Now Is the Time to Love, For the Love of Marriage*.

Drescher has written for more than 100 magazines. He has served in conventions, retreats, and seminars, in spiritual and family renewal in the United States and in many other countries. He taught for a decade at

Eastern Mennonite Seminary in Harrisonburg, and he edited *Gospel Herald* for over eleven years.

John Drescher is married to Betty Keener. They are parents of five married children and have twelve grandchildren.

Herald Press Meditation Books

By Helen Good Brenneman
Meditations for the Expectant Mother
Meditations for the New Mother

By Susanne Coalson Donoghue
Meditations for Single Moms

By John M. Drescher
Meditations for the Newly Married

By J. Delbert Erb
God's Word for All Nations

Translated by Leonard Gross
Prayer Book for Earnest Christians

Edited by Arlene M. Mark
Words for Worship

By Vernell Klassen Miller
Meditations for Adoptive Parents

By Gerald and Sara Wenger Shenk
Meditations for New Parents

By Larry Wilson
Daily Fellowship with God

By Various Authors
Visitation Pamphlet Series
(Order toll-free: 1-800-759-4447.)

Date Due

6-14-98			
10-4-98			

Code 4386-04, CLS-4, Broadman Supplies, Nashville, Tenn.,
Printed in U.S.A.